LIFE'S GREATEST TRIP

ARTHUR BLESSITT

LIFE'S GREATEST TRIP

WORD BOOKS, Publisher
Waco, Texas
London, England

TABLE OF CONTENTS

LIFE'S GREATEST TRIP

One of my favorite passages of Scripture is, "Therefore, if any man be in Christ, he is a new creature: old things are passed away; behold, all things are become new" (2 Corinthians 5:17, KJV).

Not long ago, the Beatles arrived at the London Airport to meet the Maharashie, the transcendental meditation evangelist from India. As the Maharashie stepped off the airplane, the Beatles shook hands with him and bowed low. Their words were quoted around the world: "We recognize that within us is the need for a deep spiritual experience." This was a frank and public admission that in the midst of all their fame, popularity, wealth, and sex appeal they were living in a spiritual vacuum. They were saying, "We need a deep spiritual experience."

Perhaps this statement by the Beatles is the most representative statement made by anyone about today's generation. The Beatles were looking through the empty void of material success . . . looking through the vanity of fame . . . looking through all the instruments and gadgets of amusement, the clothes, the travel, the drugs. They were saying, "We need something on the inside of us."

This plea from the Beatles to the Maharashie for a deep spiritual experience is echoed around the world by millions of young people today. You can see them on the beach, milling around in the night clubs, walking the streets in a demonstration, or sitting in a high-school class. No matter where you go, the cry is the same: "Inside of me, I'm lost. I'm empty. I'm bored. I'm frustrated. I'm trying to find myself. I want to be really turned on. I want to live! The question is 'How?' "

The Beatles finally went to India in search of this "deep spiritual experience." They talked with the Maharashie. They spent hours in meditation. When I talked with them at a recording session in a Hollywood studio, they admitted failure. "Arthur," they said, "we are missionaries of love and peace. We are evangelists just like you, and yet, inside of us, we seem never to have found that love, that peace, the way you talk about having it."

So, the search continues . . . trying to find the answer.

I am reminded of the words of Jesus Christ, "You must be born again." If we are to find that peace, that love, that joy, there must be a spiritual, as well as physical, birth. You see, Jesus Christ doesn't put patches on old lives. He doesn't try to pump up a tire that has gone flat. Instead, he gives us new life, a new birth. He accepts you first just the way you are and, then, changes you at the moment of conversion. Jesus Christ can give you that deep spiritual experience.

Mia Farrow once said: "I searched for that hidden source of spiritual power." In effect she was telling us: "In the midst of my money-power, my fame-power, my sex-power—in the midst of all that I have, I am looking for spiritual power. The spiritual power to live, to be the person that I ought to be!"

10

There is a famous song by Stuart Hamblen that says: "It is no secret what God can do, what He's done for others, He'll do for you. With arms wide open, He'll pardon you. It is no secret what God can do." Most of you today do not really understand what Jesus Christ can do—the new life He can give, the love that He can give, the eternal "trip" that Jesus Christ can give. There is a spiritual strength that comes from God. When, by faith, we receive Him into our lives, He gives us the Holy Spirit, whose power "turns us on" to love.

Look around you. Observe the "trips," the "turned on" crowd, the swingers, the free, the happy living in a groovy world of peace and love. Is it really that way?

No!

It is a hassle of hate, fear, greed, loneliness, and need. We live in a land gutted with blood, guns, sickness, poverty, and other horrors.

You see the world as a scene made up of sports cars, cool chicks, beads, groovy clothes, and plenty of "bread." Yet, I can hear you say, "Hey, Arthur, lay it on me right. That isn't the score, is it? It ain't that way."

In the midst of the success of putting a man on the

moon; exploring the depth of the sea; and building a fat, successful country, we are lost. We look for the basis of life in a materialistic society of money, sex, drugs, fame, and put-ons—without success. These give a temporary life, but it doesn't last. It's like trying to catch a bubble. You see it, reach for it, and it bursts at your touch. We are looking for a bubble that won't burst. Where is it?

Dr. Timothy Leary was the early leader of the great hippie-LSD-turn-on movement. This former professor at Harvard University began to experiment with drugs that cause the mind to hallucinate. He traveled to Mexico and experimented with different forms of drugs, including LSD. He got "turned on," and Harvard University turned him out. His message for this generation was: "Young people, what you need is to tune in, turn on, and drop out."

In his movie, "The Death of the Mind," Dr. Leary looks out from the screen, points his finger at you, and says, "Tune in! Tune in to the underground generation. Turn on! Turn on with drugs, expand your mind, move out into the world of colors, movements, and dimensions that you have never seen or experienced before. Turn on with LSD and drop out of the straight society."

His words created a sensation. Everybody is using them everywhere—tune in, turn on, and drop out. Yet, what Dr. Leary was saying isn't new. For generations God has been saying, "Tune in and I'll turn you on, and free you from the slavery of sin."

You say, "Well Arthur, what do you mean 'tune in'?"

Some of us call it prayer, or getting right with God. But the word of our day is **tune in.** It means to get on the frequency, open the door, make the right connection. Let Jesus Christ come into your life.

Jesus Christ came into the world so that you might live. Taking Him into your heart can really turn you on . . . giving you His strength to truly live!

Whenever someone is converted and they are used to riding a motorcycle, I don't tell them to stop. I just say change directions. You can't say to a converted Hell's Angel, "Trade off your Harley-Davidson motorcycle and get a VW." You can't say to someone who's been staying up all night, "Now that you're saved, you've got to go to bed at eight o'clock. Come down to our Sunday school party and pop popcorn or pull taffy."

When I was called by God to preach, I said, "Lord, I'll do anything but preach! I don't want to be a big fat, sour-faced, potbellied, paunchy preacher!" Then, I read the words of Christ: "I have come that you might have life and have it more abundantly." Jesus, man, turns you on! Not off!

Out here in California, we have a group of motorcycle riders that have been converted and saved. They are former members of some of the toughest gangs around: Hell's Angels, Jokers Out of Hell, Satan's Slaves, Renegades, Chosen Few, and others. It'll blow your mind to see them still riding their choppers—but with a difference! On the sides of their gas tanks are little bumper stickers that say "Jesus Saves." They will be loaded down with Bibles in one hand, gospel tracts in the other.

Away they go! Gunning up and down the Strip for God. But, you see, that's the way it ought to be. God doesn't slow you down. He just changes your direction!

Out on Sunset Strip, we have a gospel night club, "His Place." What's a gospel night club? Well, it's like halfway between a church and a night club—and that's a dangerous place to be. We're unpopular with some Christians and some others, so we get hit from every angle.

On our door is the peace symbol with the cross on top. Through this door come over 2,000 a night. We have a waiting line outside from 8:00 p.m. to 4:00 a.m. We stamp your hand when you come in, like all the clubs, but our stamp says "Jesus Loves You." While the people are waiting we pass out gospel tracts and our special psychedelic Bibles.

Inside, it's dim. Psychedelic posters cover the walls telling about God's love. In the first large room is a ten-foot wooden cross, a piano, a couch, and some pads on the floor. There is also a black-light room with colored lights that flash and spin. The tables are low with candles in the middle and cushions around them to sit on.

You've probably been in places that have psychedelic slides and movies that flash on the walls. Well, we have them, too, only about every fourth slide has a gospel message on it. You keep seeing the Word of God about once every two minutes.

And then we have a prayer room. It's very simple . . . an open Bible and a candle sitting on a low table. Quiet and peaceful.

16

There is no charge to come into "His Place." We serve free coffee, Kool-Aid, and food. The food is donated to us by Jewish bakeries and catering services. Night after night, guys and gals come to read our psychedelic New Testaments, pray to Jesus, and chew on Jewish bagels!

At midnight, we have a soul session. There's soul music, singing, and I preach, sharing the gospel of Jesus Christ. Then we invite everyone to make a real decision for Christ. Night after night after night they come to be saved . . . **wanting** to be saved.

There is a group of Black Panthers that have been up and down Sunset Strip. Some of these fellows have caused a lot of hassles and problems. Many of us say, "Well, the thing to do about the Black Panthers, and the Bikers, and the dope peddlers, etc., is to enact stronger laws and hire more police." Friend, I tell you what we need are more soul winners that are willing to go where the people are! Even with cops on every corner, you can't control a godless society. The only hope is to turn that Black Panther to the love of Jesus Christ. You aren't going to do it in the Sunday school class, because they aren't coming. You've got to do it in a dark alley. You've got to do it on Sunset Strip. You've got to do it when you get out where the people are!

So, a group of Black Panthers had caused some disturbances at "His Place." They beat up on some of our workers one night, with chains, fists, and knives. The police came and said they'd have them arrested.

"We'll get them for assault with a deadly weapon, attempted murder, and other charges," they said.

"No," I said, "you can't put every bad guy in jail. If you did, there wouldn't even be any jailers. We'd all be in jail. The heart of man is desperately wicked. There is not one of us who is not guilty of sin."

"They'll all come back and kill you!"

"Man," I said, "you got to die sometime!"

I personally would rather go out with a knife in the gut or a gun flash, than go out with arthritis or rheumatism. Hadn't you?

I'm prepared to go and anxious to go and ready to get on the next load. I'd rather die for love and peace than I had for hate and violence.

I told every one on our staff they could either leave or

stay. "But if you stay, you've got to be willing to die for Jesus Christ."

Everyone stayed.

The next night some of the Panthers came by. I called to one of the gang named Junior and got him in one of the rooms. I reached in his coat and pulled out a knife.

"Junior, this knife can either open a letter or a guy's gut. Your hand can choke a guy to death or lift him up. You can either curse or praise God with your lips. The choice is yours. What are you going to do with your life?"

He left with tears in his eyes.

The next night he came back with Treetop. We call him Treetop because he is six feet, seven inches tall. He weighs 260 pounds and is only 19 years old. He's lived on the streets all of his life.

Junior and Treetop knelt together and prayed. They gave their lives to Jesus Christ and were converted to Christ.

It would blow your mind to see these Black Panthers, almost everyone of them in that group, converted to Christ. They each go up and down Sunset Strip with one of our psychedelic Bibles and a bundle of gospel tracts.

They walk up to a guy and say, "Here, you read." I've never seen anybody turn them down yet.

They communicate. They lay it on. These dudes are real. They have got it. They are **sincere!**

The staff of "His Place" is made up of people who have been saved and turned on to Jesus Christ. They are converts from another way of life.

Henry welcomes people at the door. He is from New Orleans and was a member of the Black Panthers. Henry was as hard and cold as you have ever seen. The night before he was saved, he hit and nearly blinded a guy in "His Place." I put my arms around him and asked him why he had done it. He broke down and cried. The fellow had laughed at Henry's girl friend being in jail. Henry's hard heart was just a cover. Henry says that from that moment "the Lord began to chisel love on my heart."

Then there's Solo. His real name is John Ganning but he used to feel all alone so he began to call himself Solo. The first night he walked into "His Place," he was stoned out of his mind. He had "speed" in his needle and the needle was in his pocket, ready to hit up again. He stayed to hear the midnight sermon and, afterward, knelt with me in my office. There, he invited Jesus to come into his heart. Getting up, Solo reached into his pocket, took out the needle, and handed it to me.

"Arthur, I don't need this anymore."

Today, he spreads the gospel by song . . . in "His Place" and across the country. People still call him Solo, but he's not alone anymore.

Solo has Indian blood, Jewish blood, Black blood, and White blood in him. We call him the "All American Boy!" If someone is prejudiced, he asks, "What kind of blood have you got in you?" The guy tells him, and then Solo says "I've got some of me in you!" He's saved, turned on to Jesus Christ. A fellow that used to be up and down the streets, he now deals in Bible and gospel tracts. He used to trip, and he's still tripping . . . but now he's on love with Jesus.

O. J. is another staff member. He was an alcoholic, one of the violent kind. O. J. was a pianist in a night club when he came to look at the hippies on Sunset Strip and wandered into "His Place." He came to criticize and left loving Jesus with all his heart. O. J.'s real name is John Peterson. Now that he is off alcohol he still needs something in his hand. So he drinks orange juice. That's how he got the name O. J. He is playing nightly in "His Place" and singing.

Another member of our staff is Jim McPheeters. Jim was a Marine who cruised up and down Sunset Strip on weekends, fighting, turning on, and getting in all kinds of trouble. One night he came in and heard a gospel group sing. God started working in his heart and he was saved. Today, he's a full-time staffer.

Then, I come to Linda.

The first time I met Linda, she was stoned out of her head with acid. She had ridden with a San Antonio and Houston motorcycle gang and then with Hell's Angels. At 18 she was really confused, gone on drugs and sex, nothing she hadn't done. The night I met her, she prayed with me, asking the Lord to come into her heart and give her a new life.

Now, working on our staff, full time, Linda is beautiful in her dedication to Christ. Her witness is really something else. When guys on bikes come over and ask her to split with them, she hops right on the chopper and takes off. When they stop, she lays the Word of the Lord on them. Her witnessing almost freaks them out!

Right now there are all kinds of television waves, and radio waves, and a variety of sounds that are in the air. You don't see the pictures or hear the sounds because you're not tuned into the right frequency. When you plug in the television set, you can see the picture and hear the sound. It is here now, but you don't see it and you don't hear it because you're not tuned in. God is speaking today just as clearly as He has ever spoken. Jesus said, "I stand at the door and knock. If you will tune in, if you'll open the door, I will come in and I will abide with you." You can be tuned in to God right now.

He will turn you on to a trip like you have never known before.

Tune into God, let him turn you on. And drop out.

Drop out of what?

Drop out of slavery to sin.

Many of you are hung up. You said you were going to be free. So, you threw away the Bible. You threw away the church. You set Christ in the corner. And you said you were going to be free to live, to say, to think the things you wanted.

But, instead of becoming free, you find yourself a slave. A slave to sin. You can't pass by a bar without wanting to go in. You can't have somebody ask you if you want some dope without taking it. You can't look at somebody without lust. You can't stay in your house without greed. You can't see somebody get something without a rush of resentment. You're not saved. You're enslaved. A slave chained by sin.

Jesus Christ will set you free. He'll drop you out.

Christ can do three things for you.

First, He can snuff out the past. Erase and forgive all your sins and set you free from guilt and fear. Jesus calls it being born again, a spiritual birth of soul.

Secondly, He can give you purpose for living and assurance of eternity. For the lost, purposeless drift he gives value, direction, and hope. You now have reason to live and a mission to fulfill. He will be with you now and in eternity. And you with Him.

Thirdly, He gives you more now than anyone or anything else in the whole world. He fills you with love, joy, peace, purpose, self-control, and power. Taking Jesus into your life is like being naturally stoned all the time and constantly loaded with the eternal love of God.

God stepped into this world in the person of Jesus Christ. Born of a virgin, lived without sin, and died for our sins on the cross. Through His death on the cross, the penalty for sin was paid. He did for us what we could not do for ourselves, providing the way of salvation and forgiveness.

Christ said, "I am the way, the truth, the life; no man cometh to the Father but by me." Eternal life is offered from God to us through Jesus Christ; by His grace we can be saved. He is not dead but alive! Raised from the dead by the Father. He lives to make intercession for you. He is the eternal connection having paid the price for you. We are saved by trusting Jesus Christ . . . not a religion, not a church, not by living a good life . . . just Him. Life is in the person of Christ.

"For God so loved the world that he gave His only begotten Son, that whosoever believes in him will not perish but have everlasting life."

His love reaches out to you to give you new life.

"For whosoever shall call upon the name of the Lord shall be saved." This is His promise to you. Christ said,

"Behold, I stand at the door and knock. If any man hear my voice and open the door I will come in."

If we confess our sins, He is faithful and just to forgive our sins and cleanse us from all unrighteousness.

Come to Him.

"Dear God, forgive my sins. I open my heart to Jesus. Live with me forever and give me a new life. I accept Jesus as my Savior and love you with all my heart. Thank you, Lord. In Jesus' name I pray. Amen."

26

Like, if you want to get high,
   you don't have to drop
            Acid.
Just pray and you go all the way to heaven.

You don't have to pop pills to get loaded.
   Just drop
         a little Matthew, Mark, Luke, or John.

Get loaded on Jesus,
   24 hours a day,
         you can be naturally stoned
            on Jesus!

Like, with Jesus,
   He can really get it together in your head
         and in your heart forever.

It's like an eternal RUSH!

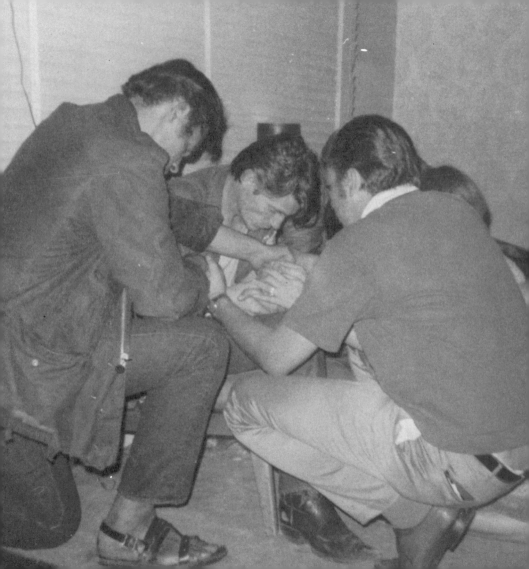

NATURALLY STONED ON JESUS

As we look at our country today, every person of every walk, background, and status in life realizes something must be done.

We look at the conditions of our time, we see the frustrations and the anxieties of our **own** lives, and we know that, **personally,** something needs to be done for us as individuals.

We realize that something must be done for our

nation—and for our world. We have got to find some way to "get it together" in our own hearts or, as many of us say, "We've got to get it together in our own heads." Not only have we got to get it together in our own heads, but we've got to get it together in the country—to be able to feel, to know, to share the brotherhood that can bind us together in a true fellowship and brotherhood.

Many times, somebody has come up to me and said, "Hey, Arthur, do you turn on? Have you got it together?"

I say, "No, man, I'm naturally stoned and Jesus puts it together forever."

Jesus got it all together in my heart one night in a parking lot, when I prayed and invited Him to be my Savior. So, there needs to be a getting together, with God, our fellowman, and ourselves.

Many of us that are trying to get the world together have come to realize that we have not gotten our own selves together. We take a glance at our world and we see the tragic and chaotic conditions of our time. Close your eyes and spin a globe—anywhere you point your finger there is a place that in a few moments could begin to usher in a disastrous World War III. Nearly every point on the globe is a place of tragedy, a place of confusion and a place of frustration.

Our world leaders have tried fervently to find a solution for peace. We begin conferences with new hopes and expectations of some formula of success only to be constantly, month after month and year after year, filled with frustration; realizing that in the midst of all our wisdom and all over brilliance, man cannot devise a way to find a solution to live together.

Not only can we not find a way to live together as nation with nation and brother with brother inside the nation, but our homes are torn with hassle, chaos, and confusion. Mothers and dads cannot find a way to communicate with their own children. There is a tremendous gap in between. Young people cannot find a way to communicate with their mothers and dads. Even husbands and wives are unable to communicate; cannot even find a way to get along. In California, one-half of those who are married wind up in the divorce courts. Fifty percent of the married couples of this state cannot find a way to live together. So, it is not only that there needs to be a getting together in the world, but there needs to be a getting together of the family. There must be a getting together of the heart.

As we look at our own country there was one time that America could stand up before the world and say, "Pattern your life after us. We are the example. Follow in our footsteps." But no longer can this be said. America now leads the world in the rate of divorce. Alcoholism is increasing in astounding proportions. The increase of drug use, "turning on" through synthetic trips, is phenomenal. The tragedy of hate and violence; racial prejudice and dissension; resentment between economic classes; deep-seated bitterness between political viewpoints; tremendous anxiety over the direction of our nation as to war or peace, capitalism and socialism; all, inward turmoils tearing America with dissension and strife. What a frightening increase in loss of unity!

Adults are asking, "What can be done?"

Young people are asking, "Is there any hope?"

At one time, many were asking the question, "Is there life after death?" No longer is that question as relevant as the question being asked by young people, "Is there life after birth? Is there anything **here** for me?"

Too many of us have looked at our own lives, have seen everything that we have, and realize that there is an emptiness, a void, that we just can't fill. Businessmen who have everything—a two-car garage, a color television set, all the clothes they need, money to travel to any place, a large banking account, savings, social security, life insurance, burial insurance, hospitalization insurance, every security a man could desire—look at me and say, "Arthur, on the inside of my heart I'm miserable, I'm lost, there's no reason for me to live. I really don't have a thing."

Many young people say, "Arthur, I've got a car, I've got my own bank account, I've got groovy clothes, all the chicks I need, everything. But on the inside of my heart I'm empty, I'm void." Many people who have everything they need go out to hassle, to destroy, to experiment with some new thing to turn on, trying to find fulfillment within their lives.

In the midst of a nation gripped with anxiety, frustration, and confusion, we recognize the need for a "getting together" in our world, in our nation, in our homes, **and** in our own heads if there is going to be any hope for our day. As I look at our world I not only see tragedy but I also see the conditions of our day as opportunities—opportunities for us to do something, opportunities for us to meet the challenge to be and receive our potential from God. This potential can make us into the person, into the society, and into the world community that we ought to be.

The Scripture says, "I can do all things through Christ which strengtheneth me." I know that there is hope.

There is a fresh breeze blowing in this land.

THE BEST TRIP OF ALL

Life's greatest trip
Is really real.
It's outa sight,
How you feel.

It's not a bummer, hassle, or hell.
It's an exciting trip,
When you know
All is well.

It's a life to Live.
A Purpose after death.
A Hope for tomorrow.
Real Life for today!

It's a beautiful trip,
With a strong helping hand.
Brothers! Get out!
Let's change that land.

36

Turn them on to the Eternal Trip!

A trip that's groovy,
Filled with love,
Peace and promise,
Sent from above.

So come on, Brothers!
Please, don't fall.
Turn on to Jesus,
He's the best trip of all.

DOWN THE DRAIN

Getting it together.

What do I mean when I say, we've got to get it all together?

In Minneapolis a while back, a guy was listening to the radio late one night when I was on a talk show. Listening to me talk, he began to think, "I don't have any confidence in preachers. They don't understand. I start talking and they don't even know what I'm talking about. I can't tell them I'm afraid I'll get busted. **Nobody** understands me."

Later he said to me, "Arthur, as I heard you speak, I realized that **somebody** did know the kind of person that I am. I felt like you understood my hang-ups because you work with people like me."

He went to our crusade rally on Friday night, but he didn't let himself be known to me. On Saturday night he came again. Then, Sunday morning he came to the church where I was speaking. This was the first time he had been in church in years and years. This young man was about 26 years old. After listening to me preach, he walked up to me.

"I want to talk with Arthur."

I took him to one of the office rooms. We sat down and he opened up the tragedies of his life.

He was a handsome, outstanding man, but sin had crept in and destroyed him. He had gotten turned on to a bummer. A former all-American football player, he was now an executive with a large corporation, traveling from city to city with his company. He was dealing in drugs, big drugs, thousands of dollars worth of drugs a week. Involved in prostitution, he was also hung up with the syndicate.

"Arthur, I'm losing my mind. I have about screwed my head off. Man, I'm strung out on STP and speed and that's a real heavy combination. Man, I can't cope with it. I'm out of it. I'm living with this chick. She's another man's wife. Last night when I got in from listening to you preach, he came in and shot at me. I was almost killed. I'm so deeply involved in everything there is no way for me to get out. My own head is now freaked out. My life is miserable. Arthur, there is no way out for me."

"Man," I said to him, "Jesus Christ said, 'I am the way, the truth and the life.' And there is a way out for you. And Paul said, 'I can do all things through Christ which strengtheneth me.'"

I shared with him how Jesus Christ could cleanse him. How that same Christ could come into his soul and take away his need for violence, take away his frustration and give him peace and rest inside.

"Arthur, I would give everything I have to have just a little of what you've got."

"You can."

We prayed together and when we finished praying he smiled one of the best smiles I had ever seen.

"Arthur, I'm ready to start. Let's have one of your toilet services."

(Well, we have what we call "toilet services." Whenever someone gives his life to Christ and he has drugs in his pocket, which is every night, he'll reach in his pocket, pull out a handful of reds or acid or a bag of grass, and say, "Hey, I don't need this anymore. Man, I'm strung out on Jesus now. It's all together in my head and heart. What do I do with this?"

We say, "Let's have a toilet service!" They all start to run to the restroom. The most we have ever gotten in is 18 small people!

We all pack inside and read this passage of Scripture: "Therefore if any man be in Christ, he is a new creation. Old things have passed away and behold all things have become new." Then we take the dope and put it in the john. Just as we start to mash the handle down, we sing a little song that goes, "Down, down, down, down, all my dope is gone."

All the dopers on Sunset Strip say, "Go to 'His Place.' They've got the hottest 'head' in town!" The person never does forget that moment when they flush that dope away. It's all gone and they know it. They go around and say, "I had a toilet service. Have you?" It's a mark of distinction!

One night we flushed down over 3000 caps of acid. We flush down thousands and thousands of dollars of drugs a year. We get high getting rid of the stuff!)

"Praise God."

"Okay," he reached in his pocket unloaded piles of pills!

We went downstairs to the basement of the church and into the men's restroom. We walked to the door of the little toilet section. We prayed, and as we did he began dropping the pills into the john, one after another. As he dropped them into the toilet, tears were running down his cheeks but he was smiling.

"I feel better than I have ever felt on anything. On **anything!**"

We flushed down, I don't know how much—$2,000 or $3,000 worth of drugs.

"Arthur, now what do I do? You know, I have used this for so many years now. How do I get off?"

"Jesus has already got you off."

"How do I stay off?"

"With Bible reading. Drop some of the words of God, pray, witness, get out and share Christ."

"Great, this is what I'll do. But what about all the drugs I've got at my house? What about the woman I'm living with?"

"Let's pray about it. God will work it out."

"All right."

He went home and in about an hour and a half he called me back and said, "Arthur, God already worked it out. The old lady I was living with, she split with her old man, left me a note and said, 'You'll never be a Christian and you'll never be a Billy Graham. You are too much of a sinner.' And they took all my dope! So God answered my prayer. All my drugs were gone, my old lady was out, and I've got a brand new life."

Now he is enrolling in a Bible College to study the word of God.

He told me, "Arthur, I've talked about everything else in the world. Now I'm going to start talking about Jesus. I feel like God wants me to be a preacher."

He's gotten it together in his own head and now he

can get it together with his brothers, with his company, with the people in society.

THE STRIP TRIP

It's a trip—
    the
    Strip—
far out.
Like
    Flowers,
    Guns,
    Banners,
    and
    Drunks.
Blood
    in the street,
    a
  knife!
    a
  flash!
    a
  club!
A Savior left behind.

46

It's a trip—
    the
    Strip—
a jet-fast life,
a groovy chick,
some Acid in the car.
Neon lights FLASH—
    everywhere—
    wild clothes, some Speed or Grass.

A chopper roars along the Strip.
A runaway chick stops to stare.
A kid,
    freaked-out,
    walks along,
    his hands up in the air.

A groovy trip—
    the
    Strip—
But where does it lead?

WHERE . . . Where . . . where . . . ?

WORLD'S FAIR TRIP

We were having a crusade in San Antonio, Texas, and I was down witnessing at a night club called "The Love Street Light Show & Circus." It was located right across the street from the World's Fair.

When I started witnessing in the club, a man found out who I was and I shared Christ with him. The guy told me, "Sure, you can have a service here. You can preach Sunday afternoon."

So, we had the night club on Sunday afternoon, but we didn't have a singing group.

"What are we going to do?" asked a preacher who was with us.

"Well," I said, "Let's go out and try to lead a group of singers to Christ."

So we started working the night clubs, one night club after another. Finally, we went into a club where a group of girls were playing. There were five of them. They called themselves "The Pink Panthers." They were beautiful girls, long blond hair, dark eyebrows and eyelids, pink lipstick and pink dresses, mini-skirts and black boots.

They were really on a far-out trip; drummers, guitarists, singers. And they were singing hard, acid rock music. After they took a band break, we began talking with them. Finally, before the night was over, three had prayed and really tuned their lives into Jesus Christ.

I told them, "Well we got three saved—three down, two to go. The Lord's got a majority so would you sing for us in our gospel rally?"

"We sure will!"

But they didn't know any gospel songs. They stayed up all night practicing and they learned a song called "Amazing Grace." It was the "far-outest" rock version of

"Amazing Grace" I've ever heard. They sang "Amazing Grace," two or three of their secular numbers, gave their testimony, sang some more "Amazing Grace," gave their testimony again, and sang some more rock music. As they continued to share all through the afternoon, hundreds of kids—over 800 young people—filled the inside of that night club. Hundreds gathered on the outside, front and back. We gave the invitation. Seventy-five or 100 young people gave their lives to Jesus Christ that afternoon.

The Pink Panthers are now living for Jesus Christ, sharing the gospel of Christ everywhere they go, living for Christ, turned on. They got it together in a new life. No longer are they out searching. They have got something to share. They are a living testimony. I have seen them, two years since that night. Their lives are a tremendous testimony of the life changing power of Jesus Christ. Living proof that turning on to Jesus is the best trip!

JOKER OUT OF HELL

I know a guy named Buddha.

Buddha used to ride with the "Jokers Out Of Hell" motorcycle club. I was witnessing to his "old lady" Carol one night in a semi-nude model studio and Buddha came in. He thought I was flirting with her. Buddha came up and said, "Hey, man, whatcha doin'?"

"Just, you know, laying a few words on your chick about Jesus."

"You're no preacher."

"Well, do you want to hear?" I replied. I started quoting some fast Scriptures, and he said, "Yes, you are. Split."

So I did.

A few nights later, I was witnessing to her again. He came back and I said, "Buddha, I want to tell you how you can really be saved."

He had laryngitis. Now, if you're gonna witness, the **best** time to catch somebody is when they have laryngitis! He couldn't talk back. I laid the words on him and when I got through, I said, "Buddha, let's pray right now that you can get saved."

"No man, this is not my thing."

"Then let me pray for your laryngitis.

"Well, okay."

"Let's go outside."

We went outside and I got down on my knees.

"Buddha, pray with me."

He got on his knees and I prayed just one sentence for his laryngitis—and about five minutes for his soul.

Then I said, "Okay, Buddha, you pray."

And, in as clear a voice as I have ever heard, Buddha invited Jesus Christ to come into his life.

As he got up he said, "Now I'm really a joker out of Hell, ain't I?"

NOWHERE

I once spoke at a coffee house on the West bank in Minneapolis, right next to the University. A large group had found out that I was coming to speak and the place was flooded with Christians. Normally, it was a coffee house where the "heads" hung out. With the influx of a pile of Christians coming to hear me speak, all of the regular people split.

One guy came up after I had spoken and handed me a note. "Preacher," he said, "this ain't our crowd that's here. Here's my address. You come over there if you want to. We want to find out where your head's at preacher.''

I said, ''Okay.''

He rounded up all the kids that usually hung out around this place. They were looking and searching for something to fill their lives. I walked over to the house, knocked on the door, went in, and sat on the floor. All of them gathered around, a whole **house full** of kids. As soon as I sat down they began to ask questions. Every question you could imagine!

''Who loves us?''

''Who cares for us?''

''Is the Bible real?''

''Where is God?''

''With so much hate and so much war, where is God, man?''

''I'm lonely, I'm miserable, I'm lost. What's the answer?''

As they asked questions and as we talked back and forth, some of the guys pulled out some marijuana cigarettes and began to smoke.

''Hey man,'' I said, ''you don't need that.''

"Preacher, we know where your head's at. You won't turn us in. You're here to help us."

"Well then, man, let me help you."

One guy just looked at me and began to laugh. "Man, my dad's a Baptist deacon," he said. "And he goes to church all the time, but you know, I'm so smart until I'm now totally miserable. I have an explanation for everything. I'm so smart I can destroy anything you've got to talk about but it leaves me so empty till I just don't know what to do. Let me read you this story that I wrote. I wrote it for my dad.

'Oh dad, we are all out in the middle of nowhere with our tongues hanging down and our minds all bucked out, a big wall around us, it being all hard and permanent, only time can take it away.

'Oh dad, we ain't the way we were. We are out here in the middle of no place, half way between never and half way between always. Just me sitting here riding alone, not knowing where we are going and exactly what we are doing, except to just keep moving.

'Oh dad, ain't we out here in the middle of nowhere with that swirling stuff around on the outside making splashes of rock and fire. The sky don't look no brighter than it did the day before. They say if you look up enough in the sunset, you can see the red blood floating across the dark sky, that big orange sky just clamoring there by the sea with death.

'Oh dad, ain't we out here in the middle of nowhere, just gliding ourself along like God in getting power to move on from other people's movements. Just like a marble.

'Oh dad, ain't we out here in the middle of nowhere? Sure it is lonely, dad, it is empty country all around here and you can see just as far as you want. But you have to stop. Your eyes get tired looking that far dad. Ain't no fences out here in this country. Ain't no animals that I can see. Maybe they live further down the imaginary road that we are following. Maybe they have just been hiding from us because they are scared we won't like the way they look or maybe they won't like the way we look.

But we haven't stopped to ask. How could anyone know dad?

'It's lonely way out here in the middle of nowhere. "Nowhere." '

"Nowhere. There is no God. There is nobody that understands me. There is no hope. No hope at all. Out here in the middle of nowhere."

We stayed up all that night and talked and shared and opened our hearts to one another. But, even as I left, I left him still sitting out in the middle of nowhere. He had everything; he had nothing.

There needs to be a getting together within our own hearts in order to get it together in the world. Where? Everywhere. Who? Everybody. Like the dopers, like the prostitutes, like the Black Panthers, the businessmen, the housewives, the high school teenie-boppers . . . everybody, everywhere.

All into one, big, beautiful bundle.

MOVING
AIN'T ALWAYS GROOVING!

Do you ever wonder—
   When skies aren't blue—
If by your own strength,
   You'll make it through?

Do you ever think—when you're all alone—
   Lot of moving . . . little grooving—
Blank faces in a sea of experiences all the same,
   On and on and on . . . .

Lost, in concrete and steel.
   A haze—a maze—a gaze.
Man, like buttons pushed, he moves.
   He moves but he doesn't groove!
Cause, moving ain't always grooving.

GETTING TOGETHER WITH GOD

I was in Dallas, Texas, a while back, and went to visit a friend. As we were talking, he was telling me where the sin was in town.

Now, when I get to a town, I go to the most sinful places anybody can ever imagine. Some people say, "Arthur, why do you always go to the worst places?" Well, I figure everybody else is going there anyway, so why should the preacher stay away?

62

Many of us are living like we are afraid that if we really have anything, we are going to lose it. What we need to do is be **insulated** and not **isolated** from the world.

My friend was telling me about this house of prostitution, a $75,000 to $80,000 home, located in the richest part of Dallas.

I said, "Man, let's go."

"Me go? I can't go down to that house of prostitution. I'm a businessman. I've got a good reputation. I can't take a chance."

"Well, if you can't go, you take me down to it."

So we drove to it and right up into the driveway.

I said, "Come on, man, come along with me."

He said, "Let me use another name."

"Man, you don't want to use another name. Somebody might find you're lying and you'll **really** get your head snuffed out. Just come on."

"Well, I'll just use my first name."

So we got to the door and I knocked and rang the buzzer. A lady came to the door and asked, "Why are you here?"

"I'm here for the right purpose," I said. She looked at me and said, "Well, come on in."

I squeezed my Bible in my pocket and walked inside.

As I sat down, most of the girls were all gone and there was just one man sitting there on the couch. I started making conversation with him, planning to wait till after all the girls came out and the men had gone before we started witnessing. Actually, we wanted a chance to witness to all of them, but we were afraid we'd be thrown out before we had a chance.

The guy sitting there said, "Man, I drink too much." It was like waving bloody meat in front of a lion. I **had** to talk to him about the Lord.

"Really?" I said.

"Yeah, and I just don't know what's happening to me. I'm getting worse and worse."

"Sir, let me tell you how you can have a new life."

"How's that?"

"Give your heart to Jesus Christ."

Suddenly, he panicked. "Oh, man, please don't bust me, please don't bust me. I'm taking my law exams next week. Please don't have me arrested!"

"Man, I'm not going to arrest you. I'm a minister." I started quoting Scriptures to him and in a minute he said, "You **are** a preacher. What are you doing in here?"

"We're here to witness."

"Well, witness." So we started sharing Christ with him.

Well, in a little bit, the girls came back out with their clients. Some of the guys came up and asked him if he weren't going to go to the back with one of the girls.

"No, I want to go home."

We gave him a stack of tracts and he went on out.

I scattered the tracts around the inside of the house. Soon, one of the girls walked up to us. She had a big "question" tract in her hand.

"What's this thing?"

"It's a gospel tract."

She looked at it and laughed, "Where in the world did this thing come from? What's the Lord doing in a place like this?"

"Well, they came from me. We have them printed."

"You have them what?"

"We have them printed."

"Are you religious?"

"I'm a minister. We came to talk to you about Jesus."

"Just a second," she said. She went out and got the madam. The madam came up and asked. "What's your business?"

"Jesus. I want to share with you how you can really get it together in your own heart. How you can have a new life and a new birth, meet the needs of your own soul and be clean."

She looked at me for a while then said, "You can stay."

We stayed there all night talking to one girl after another, and with each man that came in. We shared the gospel of Christ with everybody.

Finally, as the sun was coming up, we knelt in the living room with one young girl. Tears were flowing down her cheeks. She cried and she prayed. "Jesus Christ, make me clean. Make me pure. Make me holy. Save my soul and give me a new life."

Another girl came up and grabbed her by the hand and tried to drag her away. But she refused to go. Instead, she gave her life to Jesus Christ. She quit that morning, packed all her clothes, and walked out the door to a new life.

That's getting together with God.

WHAT HAVE I GOT TO LOSE?

A lone, lonely soul.
But, too bold
To let others know
What I hold
Inside of me.

They will laugh.

I can't take it yet.
But I can't make it either.
So maybe I'll try.
Or is it worth it?
After all, all I've got to lose—is me!
Out there—really swinging!
Bubble gum and all—
Surf and sea—   Yet . . .
Free   So lost.
Free   Too much
Free.   To lose.

MARTY

Then—I think of a girl named Marty.

I was speaking at Freedom Hall in Louisville, Kentucky. 24,000 kids had gathered to hear me. After I had finished preaching, I went back to the counseling room. A girl had waited and waited to talk with me. Finally, after I had finished talking to the group at the back and with individuals, she came up to me.

She said her name was Marty.

"Can I talk with you?"

"You sure can."

Marty put a string of beads around my neck and said, "I want you to have these beads. I'm a topless dancer. I've been working down at the Rooster Tail, here in Louisville. I'm also a prostitute. I'm also a professional pool hustler. I'm strung out on dope. Can Jesus do anything for **me?**"

"Marty, Jesus can give you a brand new life."

Marty knelt with me and prayed.

It took a long time to show her but I shared with her 1 John 1:9: "If we confess our sins he is faithful and just and will forgive us our sins and cleanse us from all unrighteousness."

Marty just couldn't believe it.

"Arthur, I can't be cleaned. I'm nineteen years old. There's no way for me. There's nothing I can do. I don't **know** anything but topless dancing. I can't work at another job. I've got no friends, nobody cares. I'm unwanted."

"Marty, Christ **can** give you a new life."

Marty prayed, gave her life to Christ, and quit her job.

But, we left town to come back to the Strip and Marty was alone, struggling. She had nobody to follow-up with her. The people who tried to follow-up with her knew nothing about her **kinds** of problems. So, in a few weeks, she was back to topless dancing. Back to prostitution. Back on drugs. Back to pool hustling.

She finally called me on the telephone.

"Arthur, I gave my life to Jesus Christ. I **can't stay** in this life. I have Jesus in me and I **can't live** the way I used to. There is nobody here in this city that understands me. What do I do?"

"Marty, do you have enough money to come out to California?"

"Yes."

The next day she flew into Los Angeles.

That day was a day that changed her life. From that day on she found friends that would help her to grow. Marty had no place to stay, so she moved into our home. She lived with Sherry, my wife, and me for several months.

Day by day we helped teach her the Word of God. We helped her to grow stronger and stronger and stronger in Christ until, now, she is a living testimony of the power of the Lord Jesus Christ.

She lives in Los Angeles with a Christian family. She has a job. She's off drugs. She's not hustling. She's not in prostitution. She's not a topless dancer. She's one of the loveliest young ladies I have ever seen in my life. She is a soft, compassionate, beautiful woman. Changed by the power of Jesus Christ.

She got it together. If **she** got it together, **everybody** can get it together.

LOUIE

A guy I know in Hawaii rides with a motorcycle club called the Alihe. It is the Number One motorcycle club in Hawaii.

Alihe means the elite, Number One.

The guy's name is Louie.

One night, I was witnessing down on Hotel Street in Honolulu during a crusade.

Hotel Street is known for heavy drugs, prostitution, homosexuality. It is a **very** rough street.

As I was walking along the street, a guy rode up on

his big motorcycle. A big, cut-down, Harley-Davidson chopper. About a $2500 machine. I hollered at him.

"Hey, brother, come over a second."

He wheeled his bike over to the side.

"What do you want, man?"

"I want you to know Jesus."

And he sat there and listened as I shared Christ. I told him who I was and began to talk about bikers; some of the bikers that had been converted.

"Yeah man," he said, "I heard about you. You work with the Hell's Angels, Jokers Out of Hell, Satan's Slaves, The Renegades, all the bikers. Come out Sunday and have dinner with us. We meet every Sunday morning. We'll stay till you get there and let you meet all the boys in the club."

So Sunday, at noon, my wife and I, and a minister that was coordinating our crusade in Honolulu, went out and had pizza with the club. We shared the gospel with the entire motorcycle club of the Alihe and they agreed to come to the crusade services on Thursday night.

On Wednesday night, Louie called and said he was in trouble. We went down in the middle of the night and talked to him and helped him with the problems that were hanging him up. But, he still wouldn't give his life to Christ.

Then the next night, when all the Alihes had planned to come, Louie was the first motorcycle rider up on his chopper. He got off and walked into a church for the first time in his life. He was 30 years old, had never been in a House of God in his life, and knew hardly anything at all about Jesus Christ. He had grown up on Robberson Island in the Pacific. It is a privately owned island where no one can even speak English. There's no reading, no writing, no radios. There is no "civilization" whatsoever on Robberson Island. He was one of the few that had left the island, come into Hawaii, but had never been to church.

Louie was a short, thick guy, at one time one of the top surfers in the country.

After we gave the invitation, Louie took us by the hand, the preacher and me, and said, "I want whoever this is that you are talking about, that can give me a new life."

We sat down and, in the simplest terms, explained

who Jesus Christ was; how Christ could give him a new life.

He put his trust in Jesus and prayed, giving his heart and life to Christ. He got up smiling. He stood there in front of the service and gave his testimony for Jesus Christ.

Then Louie wanted to go around and witness with us. He was really turned on! But when we would go up to someone and witness and ask "Would you like to give your heart to Christ?" if the person turned to walk away, Louie would grab the man by the shoulder.

"Man, listen to this guy," he'd say. "He ain't trying to beat you up, he ain't trying to hassle you, man, he's trying to **help** you. Listen to him."

We had problems with Louie trying **too** hard!

He'd say to me, "Now man, nobody's going to turn you down. You can go anywhere you want in this town and I'll go with you and all my boys will all go with you!"

Louie got all the bikers together, gave his testimony.

The next day after he was converted he came to church. We were supposed to meet him at noon to help him with Bible study.

The church was locked. The police saw Louie standing there on the church property and knew that he was there robbing. Seven policemen got out of their cars. They were going to arrest him just for standing on the church property because they knew his reputation. They had their clubs loose when they came up but Louie just said, "Man, I'm at the House of God. Don't bother me. Hey man, I'm going to study the Bible. The preacher is going to teach me the Bible." Finally, the police called the preacher's wife and she said, "The preacher's on the way to church now. Don't arrest him!"

It just blew the mind of the whole Honolulu police force when Louie was converted!

MY GIRL
IN THE COSA NOSTRA

I was preaching in one of the largest cities on the West Coast. One night, in the auditorium, a girl stepped forward.

"I want to talk."

We talked with her about her personal relationship with Jesus Christ.

"I came here hoping that there was hope for me," she said. "I've got everything, but I need something else.

Even though I'm stoned now, I can still understand."

As we shared Christ, she began to believe that she could really trust me. She said that her family was involved in the Cosa Nostra, and that she, too, was a part of the syndicate. She was moving drugs to Los Angeles. It was her main run. She was involved in everything you could imagine, so deeply involved with the Cosa Nostra that she knew that there was no way out for her.

Finally, she agreed to give her heart to Jesus Christ. We prayed together. She was saved and Christ changed her. We began to correspond with her through the mail; writing to her, sending her material. She was baptized in a local church and became active in the church.

Then she went to California to see her boyfriend that she had been involved with in drugs. He was also converted and they were married in a church service.

Both of them got out of drugs but they came to me and said that they were going to be killed for leaving the syndicate. We prayed together and asked that God would watch over them and protect them.

God did. He worked it through. They were allowed to leave the syndicate and live!

Now they are sharing the gospel of Jesus Christ in the same city that they had been dealing drugs out of. They opened a small home in that city to take in girls that are strung out on drugs. They are living a life of change and commitment to Christ.

She had been able to personally share Christ with some of the leading underworld figures on the West Coast.

She is a **living** witness to her own family.

She got it together and now she is turning others on to the same trip.

THOUGHTS

SOMEONE
Someone to care more—
   to understand.
Someone to love with—
   to feel every pain.
 Dark the late night—
   cold the day.
Wild the west wind—
   someone's lost the way.

SOMEWHERE
Looking
Wishing
Searching
Somewhere—I don't care.

Tune me in
Turn me on
Let me go
Somewhere—I don't care.

SOMEHOW

Me hung up?
At heart
Some days I say it's not real,
But yet I know—it is.
I've bruised my heel.

My Soul—my Life—my Way
Somehow I've lost.
Is there not, for real,
For me, a new day?

THERE
There is a Life—
   That's where it is—
He shed His Blood
   For you and me.
Yes, He came down—to die.

Yes, there is a Life—
   He bought it.
Receive Him now
   And Live.

Jesus, Here I am
   Here's my heart—
Hold me!
   Mold me!

GLOSSARY

Junk	heroin
Junky	heroin addict
Pusher	seller of narcotics
Mainliner	an addict that injects drug directly into vein
Pad	house or apartment
Crashpad	house or apartment open for anyone to come in and spend the night
The Man	police officer or head of any "establishment" enforcement agency
The Heat	police (singular or plural)
Nark	narcotics officer with police department
M	morphine

Booze .... any alcoholic beverage
A hit .... shot of drug in the vein
Connection .... supplier of drugs or an individual who will put you in touch with a seller
OD .... overdose of drugs
Popping .... taking drugs in pill form
Hooked .... addicted to drugs
Loaded .... under the influence of a drug
Stoned .... heavily under the influence of drugs to the point of unconsciousness
Grass .... marijuana
Weed .... marijuana
Roach clip .... a device to hold a marijuana cigarette so that it can be smoked down to the end, usually made with a paper clip
Joint .... marijuana cigarette
Speed .... methadrine, a drug that stimulates making the mind and body reactions "speed-up," can either be shot into vein or taken by capsule
LSD .... lysergic acid diethylamide; effect of drug may last from 8 to 12 hours, depending on tolerance and amount taken; effect may suddenly reoccur at any time
STP .... psilocybin, drug made from peyote buttons, much stronger drug than LSD, trips of shorter duration but wilder
Downers .... various pills that affect the mind and have

the feeling of slowing a person down, cause sleepiness, slow respiration, often cause face to turn red, speech becomes slow, pills also called "reds"

Uppers ....various pills that cause fast heart beat, racing mind, fast movements, great excitement, pills also called "whites"

A rush ....the feeling when drug quickly fills the bloodstream after injection into the vein

Trip ....period of time when person is under influence of drug, usually associated with LSD or similar hallucinogenic drugs

Freaky ....acting afraid or unusual, anyone who is easily excited, also one who is often heavily under the influence of drugs

Up-tight ....being very angry; overly concerned about something; a close friend or one you can depend upon; i.e., an "up-tight" friend

Bust ....a police raid or arrest

Busted ....being arrested

Tank ....jail

Cold turkey ....withdrawal from drug addiction without any medication to ease pain

Burn ....to sell imitation drug as real product; i.e., an aspirin for a LSD tablet

Burn artist ....one who sells imitation drug

Fix ....dose of drug, usually designates a full injection into vein

High .... the feeling one gets when on drug that stimulates

H .... heroin

Chick .... girl

Trick .... to have sexual experience with another

Hooker .... female prostitute in bars or on streets

Roll .... to steal someone's money directly from his person, usually after having sexual experience or after beating victim

Love-in .... an informal gathering of young people in park or on beach, usually with music, food, etc.; not necessarily including any activity of a sexual nature

Head .... a heavy user of drugs, especially LSD; the leader of any group

Happening .... a spontaneous gathering or experience

Bummer .... bad effect from drug; bad experience

Acid .... LSD

Snuff out .... to kill someone

Bread .... money

Straight .... conforming to regular, adult, or old-time social mores; being a member of the "establishment"

Vibrations .... feelings or thoughts emenating from an individual, no words or actions necessary

Biker .... one who rides a motorcycle, usually with a club or gang

Old Lady .... girl friend of a motorcycle rider, usually his common-law wife

"property of"	phrase refering to girl friend of motorcycle rider, often seen written on leather jackets
Lay it on me	request to give someone something; request to talk frankly or pointedly
Split	leave a location
"my thing"	phrase meaning the individual is acting in a manner natural to him; doing what one wants to do
Rap	talk
Groove	feel something deeply
Naturally stoned	happy and feeling good without the use of drugs
Pot	marijuana
Pot party	social gathering to smoke marijuana
Psychedelic	anything that affects the mind, usually associated with art and color, extremely modern in technique
Square	not in step with the "modern" moral or social mores
Hung-up	addicted to drugs; addicted to anything; i.e., a certain subject that constantly preys on the individual's mind
Turn-on	taking a drug to feel good; being happy; being made happy by anything, such as music, art, a party, or even another person
Cop-out	run away from something; to tell on another

92

Hassle ....fight or argue; to frighten or move away, usually by police or anyone representing authority